T0194291

BEAUTIFULLY BROKEN

Maintaining Faith during Difficult Times:
40 Day Devotional

K. HOWARD

WESTBOW
PRESS®
A DIVISION OF THOMAS NELSON
& ZONDERVAN

MSG:
• Scripture taken from The Message. Copyright © 1993, 1994, 1995, 1996, 2000, 2001, 2002. Used by permission of NavPress Publishing Group.

WestBow Press books may be ordered through booksellers or by contacting:

WestBow Press
A Division of Thomas Nelson & Zondervan
1663 Liberty Drive
Bloomington, IN 47403
www.westbowpress.com
1 (866) 928-1240

ISBN: 978-1-9736-5170-3 (sc)
ISBN: 978-1-9736-5169-7 (hc)
ISBN: 978-1-9736-5171-0 (e)

Library of Congress Control Number: 2019901090

Print information available on the last page.

WestBow Press rev. date: 02/22/2019

Stronghold of Unbelief

Today is the beginning of a forty-day journey that I pray finds you on the fortieth day; more empowered, abandoned to the gospel, and resurrected in the dead areas that need to rise. I too have struggled; as a believer to wrap my head around all the gospel has offered me. This includes from the beginning of my first revelation moment with God to the seasoned moments when He feels so familiar to me that I truly believe He is with me always. I could not be more blessed to know that we are walking this journey together. Today, I can boldly say that God does not let us down. Life and people may, but God will not.

Why do we need to be empowered? We all get tired and just plain worn out by life's ways of testing our tenacity, endurance, and perseverance. This can lead to years of the "Fake it until you make it" mentality as well as feelings of inadequacy, confusion, and fear. God has provided us with so many encouraging and empowering words in the Bible that we have no reason to feel lost or confused for long. We have this resource with all the answers: God's word. The Bible is our instruction book through this journey we call life. When we are empowered by the gospel, it becomes a continuous force that gets us through those moments we didn't think we could make it through.

Abandonment to God's promises in the Bible is an expression I pray leaves our lips daily as we dig into what God says to us about those promises. We may feel abandoned by the people in our lives, but God's word says He never leaves us (Hebrews 13:5). With just that promise, we can stand stronger against the situations life throws at us. God is everything He says He is, but if we doubt, we crumble in the areas where we already have victory. Maybe it's not that we don't believe the promise entirely but that we just didn't believe what God said in that moment. Know this: we can stand only on the promises we believe.

Do you believe? Do you believe Him? Do you believe what God's word says about Him even when it doesn't look like the situation turned out the way you thought it should have? Answering yes to all those questions is pivotal to receiving the benefits that are already yours if you believe.

Pray This

Dear Lord, help me with my unbelief. Help me set aside time to read Your word and gain understanding of who You are to me and who I am to You, amen. I realize I can't trust You if I don't know You. Lord, I don't want to just know *of* You—I want to know You including Your voice, character, and the things that make You who You are. I want all of You.

Meditate on This

Don't be obsessed with getting more material things. Be relaxed with what you have. Since God assured us, "I'll never let you down, never walk off and leave you," we can boldly quote, "God is there, ready to help; I'm fearless no matter what. Who or what can get to me?" (Hebrews 13:5 MSG).

Challenge

Personalize the verse with your name in the blanks.

I will not be obsessed with getting more material things. I will be relaxed with what I have. Since God assured me, "I'll never let you down, _____, and I never walk off and leave you, _____," I can boldly quote, "God is there, ready to help me; I'm fearless no matter what. Who or what can get to me?"

Journal Notes

Journal Notes

The Stronghold of Sin

Yesterday, we discussed unbelief and how that affects our faith and receiving the blessings that are already ours for the taking. Today, we will face what the Bible refers to often as sin. It has a long list of attributes connected to it, and the Bible is clear that we all sin (Romans 8:23). Considering that sin is mentioned more than four hundred times in the Bible,[1] it is probably something we shouldn't pretend is just our little issue. This is especially true since the mention of sin is always coupled with the consequence of death and total separation from God for eternity. The impact on our faith is significant.

So I have no desire to list the sins in our lives. We know what we struggle with. The hard part is facing it. But for the sake of learning about sin, let's define it.

> Sin: noun: sin; plural noun: sins; an immoral act considered to be a transgression against divine law.
>
> verb: sin; third person present: sins; past tense: sinned; past participle: sinned; gerund or present participle: sinning; offend against (God, a person, or a principle)

Love is mentioned a little more than 300 times in the Bible. But this is the "aha!" moment of the day: God is love, and if He is mentioned 4,444

---

[1] (http://www.christianbiblereference.org/faq_WordCount.htm),

times in the Bible, we know He has the power we need to conquer our sin. Sin is not unique in the eyes of God, but we are. We are absolutely precious in His sight. If God wins us over, He also wins over our sin, and the love story never ends.

Pray This

Lord, help me to focus on God's love to trump my sin. I can do this if I keep my eyes on You. Sin does not have to rule in my life if I let You rule over my life.

Meditate on This

> For there is no difference between us and them in this. Since we've compiled this long and sorry record as sinners (both us and them) and proved that we are utterly incapable of living the glorious lives God wills for us, God did it for us. Out of sheer generosity, He put us in right standing with Himself. A pure gift. He got us out of the mess we're in and restored us to where He always wanted us to be. And He did it by means of Jesus Christ. (Romans 3:23 MSG)

Challenge

The above scripture mentions "us" and "them." Us is whoever is reading the verse, and them is whoever we are comparing ourselves to. They are struggling with stuff too.

The challenge for today is to include yourself in the victory over sin set before you. Though you may struggle, don't quit. Focus on God's promises.

Journal Notes

Journal Notes

The Stronghold of Unbelief

I wonder why it takes some people so long to believe while others grab hold of the truth and believe right away. We really are all so different. Unbelief robs us of true freedom from the things in our daily lives that seem to take up so much time with very little satisfaction.

The one thing I remember most when I first believed—and now—is that when I believed what God said about Himself and what He said about me, my burdens were lifted.

Believing is so much more crucial to our walk than we sometimes give it credit for. We cannot move forward with the perfect plan God has for our lives and receive the favor and blessings that come with it if we do not believe.

We all struggle with unbelief at different times in our lives. The one place we want to root unbelief out of is who Jesus is, what He did, where He is now, and His promise to return. These are the non-negotiables of our faith. We must keep unbelief out of the areas of where we stand with Jesus. "Creed," a song written by Rich Mullins, caught my attention early on in my walk. I'd like to share it with you for our application time today.

Pray This

I believe You, Lord. I believe every word that comes out of Your mouth. I believe. Let this song minister that truth to me in a way that strengthens my belief and weakens my unbelief. Remind me that I apply only the parts of the Bible I believe, amen.

Challenge

Line by line, ask yourself these questions: Do I believe He is? Do I believe He has? Does my life reflect what I say I believe?

Use and meditate on the lyrics of this song until they resonate in your spirit and stir up a refreshing of your belief of who He is and what you determine to believe. Then apply these beliefs to your everyday life.

> And I believe that what I believe
> Is what makes me what I am
> I did not make it, nor it is making me
> It is the very truth of God and not
> The invention of any man.
> Chorus from "Creed," by Rich Mullins

I highly recommend listening to the whole song and letting it get down in your "knower."

Journal Notes

Journal Notes

Stronghold of Sin

We tend to believe that we suffer because of our circumstances and if they would only change, we'd be able to act right. But God wants us to become so mature and stable that we act right even when none of our circumstances are good.

—Joyce Meyer

I read this quote from Joyce Meyer and thought, *That is a key to dealing with our sin nature.* We focus on the circumstances to change so we can become more stable, yet circumstances are always changing, so that's not where stability lives. Allowing our circumstances to mature us is a little more accurate because life lessons mature us by how we react to the circumstances. However, I don't get a sense of stability in the middle of all that.

The reality is that maturity and stability come from an understanding of whom we lean on in our circumstances as well as whom we learn from regarding how to respond or react to our circumstances. It's a process of letting go of sinning and grabbing hold of and taking personal responsibility in the situation.

We face making the best decisions during our circumstances despite what might feel good at the time. We can feel good or do good—the choice is ours. Just a little sidebar here: these moments are a reminder of how free we are. We get a choice every time at this crossroad that says, "Will you do what feels good, or will you do what's right?" Our relationship with God is based on our want to, not our have to. He wants what's best for us, but He loves to see us choose what is best for us. Maturity and stability come when we decide it does.

Pray This

Lord, help me while I take control over the circumstances in my life by letting You take control over my life. Help me want to do what is right, amen.

Meditate on This

"But be doers of the word and not hearers only, deceiving yourselves" (James 1:22).

Challenge

Read James 1:21–27. Make a commitment to apply the principles in these verses. It's between you and God. I recommend journaling this. It's a process, but the journey is phenomenal.

Journal Notes

Journal Notes

Stronghold of Unbelief

How do we deal with our unbelief? I think we can simplify our response by believing God and His Word as it comes into our lives and making it a lifeline of hope in every circumstance, trial, and challenge that comes our way. We should simply believe.

The first time *believe* is mentioned is in the exchange of God making His covenant with Abraham in Genesis 15:6. The word *believe* in Hebrew is the root word *'aman*, to establish or confirm. It is also where the English word *amen* comes from. When we believe what God says, we establish what our minds will accept and confirm our belief with how we respond to the circumstances, trials, and challenges we face. The covenant between Abraham and God was established and confirmed when Abraham believed what God was committing to do for Abraham.

Fast forward to John 3:15, the first mention of eternal life in the book of John: "Whoever believes in Him should not perish but have eternal life." This precedes John 3:16, the verse most people have heard at least once or have seen written on signs in sports arenas around the world. Here, we move from the very personal encounter that Abraham had with God to His personal encounter with us. Our eternal life is pending on our belief in Jesus and what He did for us. When we believe God, we decide to treat His Word as certainty, commit to doing what His Word says, and apply it to our everyday life.

How do we deal with our unbelief? By believing God's Word.

Pray This

Lord, I believe you. I believe what Your Word says about You, about me, how I should live my life to get my best right now, and how to get to eternal life with You.

Challenge

Read and believe what John 3:15 says. Spend some time journaling about the areas of belief you struggle with. Find verses you can stand on to help you believe. For some of us, that will mean to help us believe again.

Journal Notes

Journal Notes

Stronghold of Sin

Today, we will look at the first mention of sin and temptation in the bible. Read Genesis 3—all of it. We will walk through from temptation to sin and to its consequences.

We learn this in Genesis 3.

- Verses 1–5 describe the serpent's temptation of Eve. Temptation is where we want to catch our sin before we act on it. Regardless of what our weaknesses are, the Bible tells us in 1 Corinthians 10:13, "No temptation has overtaken you such as common to man; but God is faithful, who will not allow you to be tempted beyond what you are able, but with the temptation will also make the way to escape, that you may be able to bear it."

- We need to apply the promises of God to our lives and live life as if we believe the promises will come to fruition. We need to study God's word for personal conviction, learning about God's character and personal revelation of our purpose as well as address our various areas of unbelief

- In verse 6, Eve and then Adam sin. Isn't it interesting that the temptation is five verses, the act of sin is one verse, and the consequences of sin are verses 7–24?

My aha moment here is this. First, temptation will come at the most inconvenient and weak moments in our lives, but God gives us a way out as 1 Corinthians 10:13 tells us.

Second, sinning is the supposedly easy part; it always comes disguised as no big deal, something everyone is doing. We think the consequences will be worth it or not as bad as God or our parents have warned us about. We tell ourselves, *It'll all work out,* but the consequences seem to unroll and we feel we're in a fight for our lives—and we are. Romans 6:23 tells us that the wages of sin is death. (Apply believe God and His Word that we learned yesterday.)

Third, eighteen verses of consequences rolled out almost immediately after Adam and Eve sinned. That is a huge number compared to the six verses combined of temptation and the act of sin. Here are my thoughts on what we can do to avoid sin and its consequences.

- Run. Run as fast as you can as soon as you realize you're in a position of weakness. Remove yourself from the situation graciously or not, but get out of there one way or another.
- Acknowledge your weakness. It will help you to avoid those situations in the future.
- Understand the schemes of the enemy—Satan. He hates you. Just know that. He has no good plan for you. He will isolate you, lie to you, mistreat you, and use others to do the same to you. Recognize these attributes and understand that Satan is the culprit and he will not rest until you are destroyed. In 1 Peter 5:8 NKJV, we read, "Be sober be vigilant, your adversary, the devil walks about like a roaring lion, seeking whom he may devour." (Apply believe God and His Word that we learned yesterday.)

Redemption is part of the scenario as well; read John 3:15–21. It is our choice to believe or not.

Pray This

I am a sinner, Lord, but You are the redeemer. I believe You. I believe Your Word. I believe I can do this with You at my side. I don't want to run from You any longer. Show me Your ways, amen.

Challenge

Meditate on this verse: "For as by one man's (Adam) disobedience many were made sinners, so also one Man's (Jesus's) obedience many will be made righteous" (Romans 5:19 NKJV).

Journal Notes

Journal Notes

Strongholds vs. God

This first week, we've focused on two strongholds—sin and unbelief—because I think getting a handle on these two strongholds is the way to uproot our other strongholds.

Sin separates us from God; its consequences are many, but the consequence that matters the most is dying separated from God for eternity. Sin's antidote is forgiveness from God (Romans 6:23).

Unbelief also separates us from God for all eternity, steals our promises, and lies to us about His existence and power. It's like sitting in a room with someone but ignoring and shutting out his or her existence and pretending it's just you there. Just as that person is real, God is real whether you believe He is or not. The antidote for unbelief is to believe God (John 3:15–21).

In 2 Corinthians 10:3–8 (MSG), Paul wrote about strongholds.

> The world is unprincipled. It's a dog-eat-dog world out there! The world doesn't fight fair. But we don't live or fight our battles that way—never have and never will. The tools of our trade aren't for marketing or manipulation, but they are for demolishing that entirely massively corrupt culture. We use our powerful God-tools for smashing warped philosophies, tearing down barriers erected against the truth of God, fitting every loose thought and emotion and impulse into the structure of life shaped by Christ. Our tools are ready at hand for clearing the ground of every obstruction and building lives of obedience and

maturity. You stare and stare at the obvious, but you can't see the forest through the trees. If you're looking for a clear example of someone on Christ's side, why do you quickly cut me out? Believe me, I am quite sure of my standing with Christ. You may think I overstate authority He gave me, but I'm not backing off. Every bit of my commitment is for a purpose of building you up, after all, not tearing you down.

Pray This

I believe You, God. Help me know and understand Your words so I can grow and fill my toolbox for living with Your tools that work in the crazy world we live in. I don't want to ignore you in the room with me any longer. I want to get to know You more. Show me how to believe. Teach me what my sins are and how I can ask for forgiveness and move forward. Thank You, God, for not making your existence dependent on my belief in You, amen.

Challenge

Read Psalm 103:12. Journal your thoughts on where you are sinning, ask God for forgiveness, and then destroy the paper. God's Word says that when He forgives you of your sins, they are as far apart from Him as the east is from the west and are no longer in His mind.

Read Revelation 21:3–7. Journal your thoughts on what you believe the Bible says about you, God, and eternity.

Journal Notes

Journal Notes

Prepare for the Spiritual Harvest

Meanwhile, friends, wait patiently for the Master's Arrival. You see farmers do this all the time, waiting for their valuable crops to mature, patiently letting the rain do its slow but sure work. Be patient like that. Stay steady and strong. The Master could arrive at any time.
— James 5:7–8 (MSG)

The Master, God, and all His promises fulfilled are our spiritual harvest. There is a ton of instruction in 2 Timothy 3:16 on preparing for the ultimate harvest—heaven. But there is a spiritual harvest we can have every day—the Spirit's refreshing. It is that newness or restart that we need to wipe yesterday's slate clean and do our best to make our right now better than our yesterday (Philippians 3:13).

We are not alone; He is always with us (Deuteronomy 31:6). Preparing for the ultimate harvest is what this time on earth is for (Proverbs 30:5). We need to trust that He is coming to bring us to His heaven, which He prepared specifically for us to rejoice forever and ever (John 14:2).

Pray This
All week, we learned about the consequences of unbelief and sin. This week, help me apply that to believing and trusting Your Word as an instruction book for life right now, amen.

Challenge

Look up the verses above in different versions of the Bible and write them out. Rewrite them with your name in them. Create prayers out of those that speak to you the loudest. End with this verse.

> If God gives such attention to the appearance of wildflowers—most of which are never even seen—don't you think he'll attend to you, take pride in you, do his best for you? What I'm trying to do here is to get you to relax, to not be so preoccupied with getting, so you can respond to God's giving. People who don't know God and the way he works fuss over these things, but you know both God and how he works. Steep your life in God-reality, God-initiative, God-provisions. Don't worry about missing out. You'll find all your everyday human concerns will be met. (Matthew 6:30–33 MSG)

Journal Notes

Journal Notes

Prepare for the Spiritual Harvest

I'm not saying that I have this all together, that I have it made. But I am well on my way, reaching out for Christ, who has so wondrously reached out for me. Friends, don't get me wrong: By no means do I count myself an expert in all of this, but I've got my eye on the goal, where God is beckoning us onward—to Jesus. I'm off and running, and I'm not turning back.
—Philippians 3:12–14 (MSG)

I agree with Paul; I don't have this all together either, nor am I implying I do. What I'm saying is that my eyes are on Jesus, eternal things, and I cannot afford to focus on the temporary things of this world. I just keep on keeping on despite what this world tries to distract me with. I keep my eyes on that goal, that is, Jesus. The only way I stay on track is if my eyes are on Him. He is the Way, the Truth, and the Life (John 14:6).

His Word is a lamp to my feet and lights my path (Psalm 119:11). Jesus is my light and my salvation—Whom shall I fear? (27:1). The Lord is my rock, my fortress, and my deliverer (Psalm 18:2). My eyes are low when they are on the path; my eyes are lifted high when they are on the throne, where my King Jesus sits. I don't need to lie low when times are hard. I need to lift my eyes to the throne and carry on, press forward, look at the well-lit path, and not look back or turn back because my future isn't there.

Pray This

Lord, teach me how to recognize You in all things and run from the things in my life where You do not hang out. I need only be where You like to be, amen.

Challenge

Read, write, and personalize this verse.

> So we're not giving up. How could we! Even though on the outside it often looks like things are falling apart on us, on the inside, where God is making new life, not a day goes by without his unfolding grace. These hard times are small potatoes compared to the coming good times, the lavish celebration prepared for us. There's far more here than meets the eye. The things we see now are here today, gone tomorrow. But the things we can't see now will last forever. (2 Corinthians 4:16–18)

Journal Notes

Journal Notes

Prepare for the Spiritual Harvest

> Don't hoard treasure down here where it gets eaten by moths and corroded by rust or—worse!—stolen by burglars. Stockpile treasure in heaven, where it's safe from moth and rust and burglars. It's obvious, isn't it? The place where your treasure is, is the place you will most want to be, and end up being.
> —Matthew 6:19–21 (MSG)

Preparing for the spiritual harvest is not a way-out way of thinking; it's about thinking of eternal things. It's about paying attention to what's important. Many times—probably most of the time—the things that weigh us down here won't even exist in heaven (Revelation 21:4), and yet we give so much thought to our daily circumstances that we can't avoid but really don't realize how temporary they are.

I totally understand challenges in life: relational, financial, parental, educational, physical—the list is endless, isn't it? Whatever keeps our minds off the spiritual harvest keeps our minds off heaven and on the temporary things here on earth that God promises will not be in heaven. How we respond to these circumstances will determine what we believe God is, who He is, and what He will do to protect us and bring us to our best outcome.

The verse above says that the place where our treasure is is the place we will most want to be and end up being. If this is true, we can say that we treasure what we think about the most, what we spend the most time on, and what we use our resources for the most often. I think you get the idea.

Preparing for the spiritual harvest is thinking about heaven, what it will be like, and learning what our purposes are here, whether we are living for our purposes, who God is, how we can get to know Him more—the list goes on. When that is our thought life and we start acting on those thoughts, we begin preparing for the spiritual harvest.

Pray This

Lord, help me keep my mind on You and the place You are preparing for me now. Let my mind not wander to the temporary things of this place but focus on the permanent things that will be in heaven, amen.

Challenge

Read, write on an index card or cards, and put this verse everywhere you are when your mind wanders off eternal things and onto the temporary things that keep your mind so busy you forget that God is cheering you on.

> Give your entire attention to what God is doing right now, and don't get worked up about what may or may not happen tomorrow. God will help you deal with whatever hard things come up when the time comes. (Matthew 6:34 MSG)

Journal Notes

Journal Notes

Prepare the Way

You're all I want in heaven!
You're all I want on earth!
When my skin sags and my bones get brittle,
God is rock-firm and faithful.
Look! Those who left you are falling apart!
Deserters, they'll never be heard from again.
But I'm in the very presence of God—
oh, how refreshing it is!
I've made Lord God my home.
God, I'm telling the world what you do!
—Psalm 73:25–28

God's presence sustains us in our challenging times and in just dealing with life daily. When we make Him our first response in times of trouble, our challenges seem to get so small in comparison to our big God. But if we focus only on the challenges, we forget God in all of it. We try to handle it all ourselves and become more overwhelmed with each moment we don't acknowledge Him in every situation. Even if we blame God for a situation, we are better off than not thinking of Him at all. He knows how we feel anyway. He wants to listen, He wants to help, and He wants what's best for us.

Pray This

No matter what I'm going through, I'm going to talk to you, first, God, before I react.

Challenge

Write this on an index card, and every time you think God doesn't care or think He can't handle what you're thinking or feeling, read this verse until you believe you!

> When they hear what you have to say, God, all earth's kings will say "Thank you." They'll sing of what you've done: "How great the glory of God!" And here's why: God, high above, sees far below; no matter the distance, he knows everything about us. (Psalm 138:4)

Journal Notes

Journal Notes

Prepare the Way

> Everything that goes into a life of pleasing God has been miraculously given to us by getting to know, personally and intimately, the One who invited us to God. The best invitation we ever received! We were also given absolutely, terrific promises to pass on to you—your tickets to participation in the life of God after you turned your back on a world corrupted by lust.
>
> —2 Peter 1:3–4 (MSG)

What does a life pleasing to God look like? The answer is simple but complex at the same time. We can list all the things we should be doing quite easily: don't lie, cheat, steal, or murder, be nice to your neighbor (even the mean ones), pray for your enemies, give joyfully—the list goes on. The complex parts are in the living that out when life throws those curve balls and we think that in this or that particular situation, we aren't expected to respond with the "life pleasing to God" list. But the reality is we are. How we respond to those difficult situations actually teaches us that the knowing of that list and the actual doing that list is where the rubber meets the road. To know to be good is all right, but to actually be good is better.

If someone claims, "I know him well!" but doesn't keep His Commandments, he's a liar; his life doesn't match his words. But the one who keeps God's Word is the person in whom we see God's mature love. This is the only way to be sure we're in God. Anyone who claims to be intimate with God ought to live the same kind of life Jesus lived (1 John 2:2–5 MSG).

Pray This

Lord, help me put into practice what you teach me through Your Word, amen.

Challenge

Put into practice what you've learned while reading God's Word. Journal about your verses and experiences and how you're doing in those areas of application. Make sure you record your wins so you can see your spiritual maturity developing.

Journal Notes

Journal Notes

Prepare the Way

> Consider it a sheer gift, friends, when tests and challenges
> come at you from all sides. You know that under pressure,
> your faith-life is forced into the open and shows its true
> colors. So don't try to get out of anything prematurely. Let
> it do its work so you become mature and well-developed,
> not deficient in any way.
>   —James 1:2–4 (MSG)

In the middle of those tests and challenges, remember that everything has its purpose but it isn't always easy to state it. Believing God is ultimately going to pour His good over all the bad isn't as easy as is letting these verses roll off the tongue. Our focus must remain on the promises and not on the tests and challenges. God says, "Anyone who meets a testing challenge head-on and manages to stick it out is mighty fortunate. For such persons loyally in love with God, the reward is life and more life" (James 1:12 MSG). So be that kind of person in this verse who begins focusing on the promises and the purpose.

I want to be so in love with God for who He is that my tests and challenges become so small in His presence that I step over them to get to Him.

The Bible will sustain you if you open it and read it as if your life here on earth were dependent on it because it is.

Pray This

I love you, God— you make me strong. God is bedrock under my feet, the castle in which I live, my rescuing knight. My God—the high crag where I run for dear life, hiding behind the boulders, safe in the granite hideout. (Psalm 18:1 MSG)

I sing to God, the Praise-Lofty, and find myself safe and saved. (Psalm 18:3 MSG)

God made my life complete when I placed all the pieces before him. When I got my act together, he gave me a fresh start. Now I'm alert to God's ways; I don't take God for granted. Every day I review the ways he works; I try not to miss a trick. I feel put back together, and I'm watching my step. God rewrote the text of my life when I opened the book of my heart to his eyes. (Psalm 18:20 MSG)

What a God! His road stretches straight and smooth. Every God-direction is road-tested. Everyone who runs toward him Makes it. (Psalm 18:30 MSG)

Challenge

Write out these verses on index cards. As life throws you tests and challenges, remind yourself what kind of God we serve. It is important to rewrite these verses throughout the readings with your name in them. Personalizing the verses that minister to you immediately will defeat the lies of the enemy in your mind. The antidote to the enemy's lie is always God's truth.

Journal Notes

Journal Notes

Prepare the Way

Give your entire attention to what God is doing right now, and don't get worked up about what may or not happen tomorrow. God will help you deal with whatever hard things come up when the time comes.
—Matthew 6:34 (MSG)

My eyes are fixed on God's plan for me. God already has a plan and solution for everything sitting in front of me and things I don't even know are about to happen. When I forget and try to handle things all on my own, that's when fear and anxiety creep in and try to convince me it's all going to fall apart. The reality is that it just might fall apart, but I don't need to react to something that hasn't happened.

In dark moments, I must count on the promise that God is the lamp unto my feet and a light unto my path (Psalm 119:105). The lamp He speaks of illuminates only about two feet in front of me; that's pretty much all I can handle sometimes when life gets so dark and downright scary. But He, the uncreated One who created everyone and everything, is shining that lamp on my path and leading me where my feet need to go. I will hold my lamp and trust that whatever lurks in the darkness must face my God. I just need to focus on the light.

Pray This
Lord, You are my only light, my only hope of surviving this dark place in my life. Help me to not lose my grip on Your lamp, amen.

Challenge

Write this verse on an index card and take it everywhere you go so you can memorize it: "God, the One and only—I'll wait as long as He says. Everything I hope for comes from Him, so why not? He's a solid rock under my feet, breathing room for my soul, an impregnable castle: I'm set for life" (Psalm 62:5 MSG).

Journal Notes

Journal Notes

Humility vs. Humiliation

So let's not allow ourselves to get fatigued doing good. At
the right time we will harvest a good crop if we don't give
up or quit. Right now, therefore, every time we get the
chance, let us work for the benefit of all, starting with the
people closest to us in the community of faith.
—Galatians 6:9–10 (MSG)

Am I the only one who thinks God and I have completely different
timelines when it comes to the right time to harvest a good crop? If we
were honest, we'd say we want a good crop any ol' time we want it, not just
when we need it. If we fully understood God knows what's best, it wouldn't
matter when we collected the harvest; we would just diligently work and
never give up because we fully understood that our harvests would come
at the right time.

We bump God out of His position with what we think is the best
timing for our situation while He patiently waits for us to humble ourselves
so He can be the provider, healer, friend, and Father we need in every
situation. It really comes down to our first week of devotions, doesn't it?
Do we believe God? Do we believe His Word? And if we say we believe,
do we live as if we believe?

Pray This

Lord, humiliate me if You have to so I can be humble enough to know my place and be content in that. I don't need to be right. I just need to be right with You, Lord, amen.

Challenge

Read, write, and pray this over yourself until it gets way down in your "knower": "The seed cast on good earth is the person who hears and takes in the Good News, and then produces a harvest beyond their wildest dreams" (Matthew 13:23 MSG).

I can't emphasize enough the benefit of personalizing these verses in the challenges each day. We want to move from memorizing God's Word to applying it. Remember that we apply only what we believe.

If you picked up this devotion, it was because you were feeling broken, going through difficult times, or just trying to build a faithful time in and with the Lord—or maybe a combination of all the above. It's time to set a new pattern in your life and get serious with your time with God so you can defeat the lies of the enemy.

Journal Notes

Journal Notes

Humility vs. Humiliation

So let God work His will in you. Yell a loud no to the Devil and watch him (the devil) scamper. Say a quiet yes to God and He'll be there in no time. Quit dabbling in sin. Purify your inner life. Quit playing the field. Hit bottom and cry your eyes out. The fun and games are over. Get serious, really serious. Get down on your knees before the Master; it's the only way you'll get on your feet.
—James 4:7–10

To let God work His will in us is a battle between His will and ours. Here's the thing—we can train our will to line up with His. It's a process, but we can learn to not sin as much, think before we speak, and give instead of receiving. We can reduce the battle of our wills against God's by following the instructions in this verse: "Yell a loud no to the Devil and watch him scamper. Say a quiet yes to God and He'll be there in no time." Sweet Jesus, that is awesome!

We need to spend as much time as we can in God's presence and Word and talking to Him. That is when we get to know Him so well that His character and will ultimately become ours. Then, when sin comes creeping in, we can yell, "Not today, devil. Not today!" and know God is right there helping us turn away from the devil's courtship for our souls and we can then spend our time preparing for the Wedding Supper of the Lamb (Revelation 19:9).

Pray This

Not my will, Lord, be done in my life but Yours. I ask that Your will be kneaded into my life so You are so ingrained in me that people experience Your presence before they encounter me. I want humility before I am humiliated trying to do everything in my own strength, amen.

Challenge

Read, write, and memorize this verse.

> You're cheating on God. If all you want is your own way, flirting with the world every chance you get, you end up enemies of God and His way. And do you suppose God doesn't care? The proverb has it that "He's a fiercely jealous lover." And what He gives in love is far better than anything else you'll find. It's common knowledge that God goes against the willful proud; God gives grace to the willing humble. (James 4:4–6 MSG)

Journal Notes

Journal Notes

Humility vs. Humiliation

> Don't fret or worry. Instead of worrying, pray. Let petitions and praises shape your worries into prayers, letting God know your concerns. Before you know it, a sense of God's wholeness, everything coming together for God, will come and settle you down. It's wonderful what happens when Christ displaces worry at the center of your life.
> —Philippians 4:6–7 (MSG)

Fretting and worrying are responses the enemy uses to humiliate us. When we are fretting and worrying about life stuff instead of looking to God and His Word and praying and talking to Him about our circumstances, we are humiliating ourselves into a tizzy of doubt, fear, and counterproductive reactions vs. proactive trust in God.

We are more than conquerors (Romans 8:37), so why aren't we acting like conquerors? If we stand right with God, we will stand righteous in any situation regardless of the outcome. The Bible says our fight is not with people but with the devil and his advocates (Ephesians 6:12), so why aren't we standing with God against the devil?

Our eyes and ears, the very senses God gave us, should always be fully attentive on God but especially when the devil is at work in our lives. Humility is the character trait we need in this moment to not focus on the person who appears to be instigating the problem, not on the problem, not on ourselves, and not on the devil. We need to humble our hearts, minds, and souls to lift our eyes to heaven so we can remind ourselves who is in charge, who will come to our rescue, and who will and has overcome this world—Jesus. We need to get out of the way of our prideful, controlling ways and let God be God in every circumstance.

Pray This

Lord, I am trading in worry and stress for Your presence and promises. I can't afford one moment to pass me by without considering Your thoughts on it, God, amen.

Challenge

Read, write, and memorize this.

> Summing it all up, friends, I'd say you'll do best by filling your minds and meditating on things true, noble, reputable, authentic, compelling, gracious —the best, not the worst, the beautiful, not the ugly; things to praise, not things to curse. Put into practice what you learned from Me, what you heard and saw and realized. Do that, and God, who makes everything work together, will work you into His most excellent harmonies. (Philippians 4:8–9 MSG)

The challenge verse for today was one of the first three verses I memorized as a new Christian about thirty years ago. I can tell you this—it's still alive and working in my life today. This verse defeats the negativity and the drama that tries to invade my life.

Journal Notes

Journal Notes

Humility vs. Humiliation

> If we claim that we experience a shared life with Him and continue to stumble around in the dark, we're obviously lying through our teeth—we're not living what we claim. But if we walk in the light, God Himself being light, we also experience a shared life with one another, as the sacrificed blood of Jesus, God's Son, purges all our sin.
> —1 John 1:6–7 (MSG)

Humility comes when we admit our sins, wrongs, and misunderstandings so God can purge those dark things in us with His light. Humiliation comes when we attempt to hide our sins, wrongdoings, and misunderstandings because in the end, our sins will indeed find us out (Numbers 32:23).

Humility admits while humiliation looks forward to exposing. When Adam and Eve sinned in the garden, God knew what they had done, but He was looking for a confession, not humiliation. He saw that they were naked, but rather than continue to expose them, He covered them. He knew they couldn't stay in paradise, but He had already prepared an alternative life for them until heaven was ready for His children. God knew that sin would separate them, but He prepared His Son, Jesus, to take on the consequences for them.

God isn't looking to humiliate us in our sin; He is looking to humble us so we can see how truly big and awesome He is. He already knows what we've done, and He already has a plan of redemption if we're willing to talk to Him about it, admit it, and let Him lead.

Pray This

I confess this to You, Lord, _____

    I ask Your forgiveness. I am laying myself at Your feet and in Your loving arms so You can help me and lead me to the plan and purpose You have for me in spite of me, amen.

Challenge

Read, write, and meditate on these verses.

> But if you don't do what you say, you will be sinning against God; you can be sure that your sin will track you down. (Numbers 32:23 MSG)

> If we claim we're free of sin, we're only fooling ourselves. A claim like that is errant nonsense. On the other hand, if we admit our sins—make a clean breast of them—He won't let us down; He'll be true to Himself. He'll forgive our sins and purge us of all wrongdoing. If we claim we've never sinned, we out-and-out contradict God—make a liar out of Him. A claim like that only shows off our ignorance of God. (1 John 1:8–10 MSG)

    Ask yourself if you're willing to tell on yourself before God, who already knows or allows sin to expose and humiliate you. I can tell you this—God is in the lighting business and darkness cannot overwhelm Him or His light.

Journal Notes

Journal Notes

Humility vs. Humiliation

Going through the motions doesn't please You. A flawless performance is nothing to You. I learned God-worship when my pride was shattered. Heart-shattered lives ready to love don't escape God's notice.
—Psalm 51:16–17 (MSG)

Humility is coming to God with our brokenness. When we try to handle it ourselves, we open ourselves up to humiliation. We were not created to handle life here alone. God created us for relationship with Him and others. God loves us, wants what's best for us, and gives us the freedom to choose while still being available to help us out of trouble when our choices are off the path of His plan for us. He is always ready, willing, and able to get us through whatever this life on earth tosses in front of us. We stumble, we may even fall, but He says in Psalm 51:17, "Heart shattered lives ready to love don't escape God's notice." The fall might be humiliating, but the lifter of our hearts lifts our spirit too.

Pride will get in the way of this beautiful exchange if we let it. Let's stop going through the motions as if we have it all together and can handle it on our own. Let's just admit with humility and recognize that we have no idea what we're doing and trust God to lead us.

Pray This

Lord, I have no idea what I'm doing, but if in my stumbling around in life I keep my eyes on You, I know I'll be okay. Help me lay down my pride and quit worrying about what others think or say and be ready to love and accept Your plan and purpose for my life as I let You take the lead, amen.

Challenge

Read, write, mediate on, and memorize this promise: "God is our refuge and strength, always ready to help in times of trouble. So we will not fear when earthquakes come and the mountains crumble into the sea" (Psalm 46:1–2 NLT).

This is how I personalized this verse: God is my refuge and strength! He is always ready to help me in my time of trouble and need. So I will never fear anything or anyone, amen!

Journal Notes

Journal Notes

Humility vs. Humiliation

GOD's there, listening for all who pray, for all who pray
and mean it. He does what's best for those who fear him—
hears them call out, and saves them.
—Psalm 145:18–19 (MSG)

These two verses are packed with wisdom, humility, and promise. Wisdom in the one who talks to God and takes the time to listen and actually hear what God has to say. Humility in the wisdom to fear God in the sense that He knows everything and understands that it's the only fear that leads to ultimate provision and protection from His hand. The promises from these verses are these.

1. God is available.
2. God listens.
3. God responds.
4. God does what's best.
5. God saves.

We can take the simplest list of God's promises and revise it in our mind to be met based only on our strengths and abilities. It's when we realize that God gave us our strengths and abilities to use for Him that we humbly take a knee and let Him lead the way. We need to talk to God about our life and needs and be quiet long enough to hear His response.

Pray This

God, help me remember that Your thoughts toward me are always good, that You are available because You choose to be out of Your great love for me, and that You always want what's best for me, amen.

Challenge

Read, write, meditate on, and memorize this passage: "For I know the plans I have for you, declares the Lord; plans to prosper you and not to harm you; plans to give you hope in your final outcome" (Jeremiah 29:11; my paraphrase from various versions).

I have declared this to be my life verse. I have looked at it, sifted it, and studied it in several versions so that it rolls off my tongue as easily as does my name. I highly recommend asking God for a life verse. It will be shown to you, and you will know it because it will speak to you so uniquely and become your standard and well of refuge.

God Is Fighting for Us

But the Lord is faithful, who will establish you and guard
you from the evil one.
—2 Thessalonians 3:3

He is faithful to see us through whatever our situation is. We often put limits on God based on our abilities and knowledge, but God doesn't need our abilities or knowledge; He is the one who designed them for us to use for and with Him. Without Him, we are limited. With Him, we are an unstoppable force.

When we wrap our mind around His awesomeness, we are released to apply what we know we're able to do and let God fill in the gaps. He wraps Himself up in love, leads us to the best places, and establishes us in peace so we can face even the most intimidating of situations.

Pray This
Lord, establish me in Your knowledge and wisdom so I recognize your lead. I don't want to miss a thing with You by my side. Help me memorize and apply Your promises. Help me learn about Your character and develop a trust for You around that knowledge, amen.

Challenge
Read, write, meditate on, and memorize this.

Fix this picture firmly in your mind: Jesus, descended from the line of David, raised from the dead. It's what you've heard from me all along. It's what I'm sitting in jail for right now—BUT GOD'S WORD ISN'T IN JAIL! That's why I stick it out here—so that everyone God calls will get in on the salvation of Christ in all its glory. This is a sure thing: If we die with Him; we'll live with Him; If we stick it out with Him, we'll rule with Him; If we turn our backs on Him, He'll turn His back on us; If we give up on Him, HE DOES NOT GIVE UP—for there is no way He can be false to Himself. (2 Timothy 2:8–13 NKJV)

On the other side of your index card, feel free to track any aha moments based on today's memory verse challenge.

Journal Notes

Journal Notes

God Is Fighting for Us

So here's what I want you to do, God helping you: Take your everyday, ordinary life—your sleeping, eating, going-to-work, and walking-around life—and place it before God as an offering. Embracing what God does for you is the best thing you can do for him. Don't become so well-adjusted to your culture that you fit into it without even thinking. Instead, fix your attention on God. You'll be changed from the inside out. Readily recognize what he wants from you, and quickly respond to it. Unlike the culture around you, always dragging you down to its level of immaturity, God brings the best out of you, develops well-formed maturity in you.

—Romans 12:1–2 (MSG)

Many of us struggle with the simplicity of this instruction in Romans 12. Sometimes, we just forget who oversees what. God is the uncreated One who created us. He is in charge of everything from beginning to end, before there was a beginning and after time is converted to eternity. We are in charge of how we respond to that.

God gave us free will, but free will in these verses comes with instructions. He doesn't want to control us but to lead us. God is such a gentleman that He won't drag us. He wants us to come along of our own free will simply because we trust Him. If we could only wrap our mind around how free we really were, the devil would never have a chance to trip us up.

Pray This

Lord, help me use my free will to trust You and let You lead. I want to experience the kind of freedom that liberates me from the shackles of worldly thinking, small thinking, fear, and lack. Help me see that as long as I have You, Lord, I have all I need.

Challenge

Read, write, meditate on, and memorize this.

> I'm speaking to you out of deep gratitude for all that God has given me, and especially as I have responsibilities in relation to you. Living then, as every one of you does, in pure grace, it's important that you not misinterpret yourselves as people who are bringing this goodness to God. No, God brings it all to you. The only accurate way to understand ourselves is by what God is and by what he does for us, not by what we are and what we do for him. (Romans 12:3 MSG)

Journal Notes

Journal Notes

God Is Fighting for Us

Keep watch over me and keep me out of trouble; Don't let me down when I run to you. Use all your skill to put me together; I wait to see your finished product. GOD, give your people a break from this run of bad luck.
—Psalm 25:20–22 (MSG)

We need to remember that when we cry out to God like this, He is already moving on our behalf. This outcry from David's mouth to God's ear wasn't necessary not because God didn't know what was happening but because He wanted David to say he knew what was happening. It's exactly the same with us; our prayers might not always be perfect, eloquent, and well articulated, but if they're sincere, genuine, and directed at God, He is delighted to hear and act on our behalf.

We do not need another well-written prayer by a professional writer; we need a raw, encountered discussion with God.

Prayer
Lord, help me open my mouth and speak to You from the heart. I need to be reminded that talking to you is about building relationship not a ritualistic way to get what I want from You

Challenge
Read, write, meditate on, and memorize this.

Or, you may fall on your knees and pray—to God's delight! You'll see God's smile and celebrate, finding yourself set right with God. You'll sing God's praises to everyone you meet, testifying, "I messed up my life— and let me tell you, it wasn't worth it. But God stepped in and saved me from certain death. I'm alive again! Once more I see the light!" (Job 33:26–28 MSG)

Write and speak to God as if He were sitting in the room with you right now because He is. Journal your experience of just speaking openly with God with no agenda in mind; just have a venting session with Him.

Journal Notes

Journal Notes

God Is Fighting for Us

I'm thanking you, GOD, from a full heart, I'm writing
the book on your wonders. I'm whistling, laughing, and
jumping for joy; I'm singing your song, High God.
—Psalm 9:1–2 (MSG)

The most difficult thing to do is to rejoice in God and who He is when
times are hard. But the more I remind myself of all that He's already gotten
me through, the more I find myself looking up instead of down. I can
feel the Holy Spirit stir in me when I'm at my lowest point and say, "But
God…", lift my eyes to Him, and list all that I've survived in my lifetime
because of God's hand on my life. Those problems shrink, hope begins to
rise, and my body eventually follows.

I choose to fix my eyes on the God who already did something for me,
and I then believe He'll do it again. I release my ways in exchange for His.

I don't need to focus on my hard times. I need to focus on being at
peace with God's timing in the hard times.

Pray This

Lord, when I feel knocked down by the storms of life, remind me to knock
on the door of Your heart, where my peace and refuge are always waiting
for me to embrace. Every test, trial, and challenge is an opportunity to see
how big You are and how big my faith can be while preparing me for the
next round of tests, trials, and challenges, amen.

Challenge

Read, write, meditate on, and memorize this: "GOD's a safe-house for the battered, a sanctuary during bad times. The moment you arrive, you relax; you're never sorry you knocked" (Psalm 9:9–10 MSG).

Journal Notes

Journal Notes

God Is Fighting for Us

GOD! Look! Enemies past counting! Enemies sprouting like mushrooms, Mobs of them all around me, roaring their mockery: "Hah! No help for him from God!"
—Psalm 3:1–2 (MSG)

When I feel that the world is crashing in on me and the people I thought had my back were the ones holding the knife all along, I have to remind myself that there's only One who truly has my back.

We put too much pressure on spouses, loved ones, and friendships to not fail us, or we think that it means they're not truly who they say they are. I'm not saying there are no toxic people from whom we need distance, but God will deal with them if we seek Him on how to handle them. I'm talking about disappointment from forgetting that people, yes, even people who love us, will fail us. It's a good thing in that moment to ask these questions.

- Did I expect too much from them?
- Did I put too much pressure on them?
- Am I letting past experience dictate my response in this situation?

It's called grace. To the same extent we lend grace, we receive it from God. How much grace do you need? I need a lot!

Pray This

Lord, You will help me distinguish between the people who have wronged me who need to be forgiven but need to go and the people who also need to be forgiven who need to stay in my life. Help me be a grace giver and boundary keeper, amen.

Challenge

Read, write, meditate on, and memorize this.

> But you, GOD, shield me on all sides; You ground my feet, you lift my head high; With all my might I shout up to GOD, His answers thunder from the holy mountain. I stretch myself out. I sleep. Then I'm up again—rested, tall and steady, Fearless before the enemy mobs Coming at me from all sides. (Psalm 3:3–6 MSG)

Journal Notes

Journal Notes

God Is Fighting for Us

I love you, GOD—you make me strong. GOD is bedrock under my feet, the castle in which I live, my rescuing knight. My God—the high crag where I run for dear life, hiding behind the boulders, safe in the granite hideout. I sing to GOD, the Praise-Lofty, and find myself safe and saved.

—Psalm 18:1–3 (MSG)

Praise is the way through any situation. It sounds too simple to be true, but it's not. It's easy to praise when things are going well, but when things aren't going as we think they should, we tend to spend our time questioning, complaining, and worrying and maybe even being grumpy, moody, and oversensitive.

But this verse from the mouth of David reminds us how important it is to praise God with confidence even when things aren't going well because in David's Praise-Lofty, he found himself safe and saved.

If we focus on the bad things happening, we quickly lose sight of God's abilities, power, and love on our behalf. Our total existence is based on His great love to be with us forever. God is wrapped up in our everything because we are everything to Him.

Focus on God, the Praise-Lofty, and you will be safe and saved too.

Pray This

Lord, forgive me for not getting in Your Word that ignites praise if I allow it to. Your Word is a great reminder of Your awesomeness in every situation. Let praise be on my lips instead of worry and complaints, amen.

Challenge

Read, write, meditate on, and memorize these verses.

> A hostile world! I call to GOD, I cry to God to help me. From his palace he hears my call; my cry brings me right into his presence— a private audience! But me he caught—reached all the way from sky to sea; he pulled me out Of that ocean of hate, that enemy chaos, the void in which I was drowning. They hit me when I was down, but GOD stuck by me. He stood me up on a wide-open field; I stood there saved—surprised to be loved! (Psalm 18:6, 16–19 MSG)

Journal Notes

Journal Notes

God, Our Promise Keeper

And this is what will happen: When you, on your part, will obey these directives, keeping and following them, GOD, on his part, will keep the covenant of loyal love that he made with your ancestors: He will love you, he will bless you, he will increase you.
—Deuteronomy 7:12–13 (MSG)

God is a promise keeper to us all, believers and nonbelievers alike. Rewards and sacrifices for believers are listed in these verses; that means there are curses and consequences for those who do not make the necessary sacrifices in their beliefs, behavior, and commitment to a God-honoring life.

God keeps His promises to the believer and nonbeliever alike. When we choose God, we choose eternal blessings. When we reject God, we reject those eternal blessings.

Pray This
Lord, thank You for knocking on my heart's door and not giving up on me. I choose You every day of my life here and when my days are exchanged for all of eternity with You, amen.

Challenge
Read, write, meditate on, and memorize this.

Then Joshua told the people: Worship the Lord, obey him, and always be faithful. Get rid of the idols your ancestors worshiped when they lived on the other side of the Euphrates River and in Egypt. But if you don't want to worship the Lord, then choose here and now! Will you worship the same idols your ancestors did? Or since you're living on land that once belonged to the Amorites, maybe you'll worship their gods. I won't. My family and I are going to worship and obey the Lord! (Joshua 24:14–15 CEV)

Journal Notes

Journal Notes

God, Our Promise Keeper

From Paul, a servant of God and an apostle of Jesus Christ. I was chosen and sent to help the faith of God's chosen people and to lead them to the truth taught by our religion, which is based on the hope for eternal life. God, who does not lie, promised us this life before the beginning of time, and at the right time he revealed it in his message. This was entrusted to me, and I proclaim it by order of God our Saviour.

—Titus 1:1–3 (GNB)

Just as Paul was, we are chosen, sent to help, and lead people in truth that is based on the good news: hope of eternal life. We can stand behind the good news of eternal life with very little effort if we don't overthink it for a few reasons.

1. Our personal testimony of how and when we believe God is who He says He is.
2. God does not lie.
3. Leading others is a natural reaction when we learn about something good.

Our testimony speaks for itself. It's the one personal experience that is not up for debate. Our testimony is the next greatest testament to Jesus's death on the cross. The day we believed, death lost its hold on us. Yes!

God does not lie; He cannot lie, so there is no lie in Him. Doubt of the good news and who God is does not come from God but from that liar, the devil, who tries to trip you up thinking you didn't "really hear what God said." Sound familiar? Read the encounter of Eve and the serpent in Genesis if you're not sure.

Leading others helps us stay grounded in what we believe, how we live, and ultimately how we walk out and grow in our faith. The key is to point to Jesus and not ourselves.

Pray This

Lord, thank You for choosing me. I choose You, and I'm not looking back. It's a new day, a new season. That devil is going to get worn out trying to chase me while I'm chasing You, God! I love You, Lord, amen.

Challenge

Read, write, meditate on, and memorize this.

> For since a church leader is in charge of God's work, he should be blameless. He must not be arrogant or quick-tempered, or a drunkard or violent or greedy for money. He must be hospitable and love what is good. He must be self-controlled, upright, holy, and disciplined. He must hold firmly to the message which can be trusted, and which agrees with the doctrine. In this way he will be able to encourage others with the true teaching and also to show the error of those who are opposed to it.
>
> Everything is pure to those who are themselves pure; but nothing is pure to those who are defiled and unbelieving, for their minds and consciences have been defiled. They claim that they know God, but their actions deny it. They are hateful and disobedient, not fit to do anything good. (Titus 1:7–9, 15–16 GNB)

Journal Notes

Journal Notes

God, Our Promise Keeper

Mary didn't waste a minute. She got up and traveled to a town in Judah in the hill country, straight to Zachariah's house, and greeted Elizabeth. When Elizabeth heard Mary's greeting, the baby in her womb leaped. She was filled with the Holy Spirit, and sang out exuberantly, You're so blessed among women, and the babe in your womb, also blessed! And why am I so blessed that the mother of my Lord visits me? The moment the sound of your greeting entered my ears, The babe in my womb skipped like a lamb for sheer joy. Blessed woman, who believed what God said, believed every word would come true!

—Luke 1:39–45 (MSG)

Mary carried our Savior and King until His little life was established. Her promise to walk this out was enough to change eternity for all who would believe that a virgin would be with child by the Holy Spirit and deliver the child who would soon deliver her, her family, and her community and touch her world and continue on long after she was gone. One single act of obedience affected so many.

There is so much to learn from Mary's obedience. First, let's look at Mary's excitement. She didn't waste a minute joining others who believed to celebrate something that had not yet been completed in her.

Second, she sang out exuberantly when the baby leaped in her womb.

The evidence of her calling to keep this child of promise safe and sound and growing and developing in her was enough to make her sing praises and stir someone else's seed! God has planted a seed in us all that needs our attention, loving care, and obedience to the end. Are you nurturing that seed planted in you to the point that it stirs in you and you cannot contain your praise?

Third, Mary believed what God had told her. She went to others who believed it too. Are you hanging out with people who help your seed grow and stir and move you to praise God while you're walking it out? Not only stir you but also to cause another's seed to leap?

Pray This

Lord, I believe You. Stir in me my praise and thanks for who You are and what You've planted in my life to nurture, love, and grow as I walk out my everyday life knowing that I am living for my extraordinary life promised for all of eternity, amen.

Challenge

Read, write, meditate on, and memorize theses verses: "When they finished everything required by God in the Law, they returned to Galilee and their own town, Nazareth. There the child grew strong in body and wise in spirit. And the grace of God was on him" (Luke 1:39–40).

Journal about how much experience you have extending grace and receiving grace.

Journal Notes

Journal Notes

The Great Exchange

But now that you've found you don't have to listen to sin tell you what to do, and have discovered the delight of listening to God telling you, what a surprise! A whole, healed, put-together life right now, with more and more of life on the way! Work hard for sin your whole life and your pension is death. But God's gift is real life, eternal life, delivered by Jesus, our Master.
—Romans 6:22–23 (MSG)

Things that pull us away from God's plan and purpose seem to be obligatory tasks that lead us nowhere but to a place where we're tired, broke, and disappointed. These tasks consume us and suck us into a cyclical pattern that uses up our time, resources, and thoughts.

How do we stop that? We want what God wants, but we don't know how to stop these patterns. This verse tells us we don't have to listen to sin tell us what to do. So the first step is to stop.

Second is to make the exchange of bad habits for good ones. We can't even start the exchange until we get to know God. We can't get to know God without spending time in His Word and presence and learning to recognize His voice over all the noise of this world.

This all sounds great, but some of us are wasting a big pile of time doing stuff that has nothing to do with what God has planned for us. It's time to start exchanging our bad stuff for good stuff.

Start with taking five to fifteen minutes a day (preferably at the beginning of your day) reading verses. I recommend reading the book of John first, then Romans from start to finish in the Message Version.

Before you do so, ask God to show you His plan and purpose for your life, ask Him to exchange every thought that leads to sin for thoughts that lead to Him, and ask Him to redeem the lost parts and open your eyes to His truth. Have a journal nearby to jot notes as you set this new pattern in your life. Give yourself time to adjust. You didn't get here overnight, so take your time and let God's Word stick and get down into your knower.

Pray This

Lord, I need to get some things, people, and habits out of my life. I want to exchange my ways for Yours. I don't realize what I'm missing with You if I'm not spending time with You. Help me guard that time I set aside for You. Remove all distractions from my mind, my surroundings, and my heart, amen.

Challenge

Read, write, meditate on, and memorize this.

> So, since we're out from under the old tyranny, does that mean we can live any old way we want? Since we're free in the freedom of God, can we do anything that comes to mind? Hardly. You know well enough from your own experience that there are some acts of so-called freedom that destroy freedom. Offer yourselves to sin, for instance, and it's your last free act. But offer yourselves to the ways of God and the freedom never quits. All your lives you've let sin tell you what to do. But thank God you've started listening to a new master, one whose commands set you free to live openly in his freedom! (Romans 6:15–18 MSG)

Journal Notes

Journal Notes

The Great Exchange

As God's partners, we beg you not to accept this marvelous gift of God's kindness and then ignore it. For God says, "At just the right time, I heard you. On the day of salvation, I helped you." Indeed, the "right time" is now. Today is the day of salvation.
—2 Corinthians 6:1–2 (NLT)

Today is a good day to exchange your sin for salvation. God hears the cry of your heart. He knows what you need and how to meet that need. He will not force Himself on you. God is patiently waiting to save you. Today is a good day to let Him.

Pray This

Lord, I ask You to take over. I give You permission, full access to intervene on my behalf. There's so much I need to learn about getting to know You, making good choices consistently, and exchanging what isn't moving me toward the passion and purpose You planted in me. Help me identify my and rest until I complete it, amen.

Challenge

Read, write, meditate on, and memorize this.

Therefore, come out from among unbelievers, and separate yourselves from them, says the LORD. Don't touch their filthy things, and I will welcome you. And I will be your Father, and you will be my sons and daughters, says the LORD Almighty. (2 Corinthians 6:17–18 NLT)

Journal Notes

Journal Notes

The Great Exchange

Do you, my friend, pass judgement on others? You have no excuse at all, whoever you are. For when you judge others and then do the same things which they do, you condemn yourself.

—Romans 2:1 (GNB)

Judging others gets us in all kinds of trouble with God and others mentally and emotionally. It's not our place to judge. If we judge others, we're actually getting into what is God's business instead of dealing with our own. When we do that, we are then judged to the same extent we judge others: "For God will judge you in the same way as you judge others, and he will apply to you the same rules you apply to others" (Matthew 7:2 GNB).

At some point, if we're judging others, we need to ask ourselves if we can afford the consequences of doing that. We have our own list of stuff God will judge, so do we really want to add judging others to our list?

I will keep this in mind: *Am I part of others' problems? Did I cause them to stumble or contribute to it in any way?* I imagine myself in the same situation and ask myself, *What would help me the most?* I need to remember that while I'm judging others, I'm not taking care of my own messes. I'm responsible only for the refection I see in the mirror. I need to first pray for others and ask God if I am to offer any advice or mind my own business and keep praying. There is no place in my life for judging others. I need to stay in my own lane at all times and let God be God.

Pray This

Lord, help me mind my own business and focus on being about Your business for my life, amen.

Challenge

Read, write, meditate on, and memorize this.

> If you sin without knowing what you're doing, God takes that into account. But if you sin knowing full well what you're doing, that's a different story entirely. Merely hearing God's law is a waste of your time if you don't do what he commands. Doing, not hearing, is what makes the difference with God. (Romans 2:12–13 MSG)

Journal Notes

Journal Notes

The Great Exchange

Oh! Teach us to live well! Teach us to live wisely and well! Come back, GOD —how long do we have to wait?—and treat your servants with kindness for a change. Surprise us with love at daybreak; then we'll skip and dance all the day long. Make up for the bad times with some good times; we've seen enough evil to last a lifetime. Let your servants see what you're best at—the ways you rule and bless your children. And let the loveliness of our Lord, our God, rest on us, confirming the work that we do. Oh, yes. Affirm the work that we do!
—Psalm 90:12–17 (MSG)

It's okay to cry out to God in frustration for what this life can offer. Sometimes, the struggle is so real and so long that it seems it will never end. But I can assure you that this life will have its beginning and its end. I can also assure you that Jesus is coming back just as He said He would. It's all going to be okay. Maybe you're asking yourself right now, *How can she be so sure?* Here's my answer.

1. He has made good on so many promises already recorded in the Bible.
2. When I focus on what He's already done, my hope of eternal life becomes more of a reality and less of an idea.
3. Getting to know His character helps me trust Him.

4. My testimony lives and breathes in me and reminds me that He saved me from many ugly things and moved me forward toward many beautiful things. I wouldn't be who I am today if God hadn't reached down and rescued me.

Pray This

Lord, let me spend my time testifying to what You've done in my life even if that means testifying to myself. I don't need any audience bigger than one. You are the only One who matters, Lord. Help me seek You first instead of other thoughts and opinions. Help me not lose sight of what You've already done in my life so that my faith in what's not been revealed is increased in trusting the outcome will be good with You on my side.

Challenge

Read, write, meditate on, and memorize this.

> Now, stay strong and steady. Obediently do everything written in the Book of The Revelation of Moses —don't miss a detail. Don't get mixed up with the nations that are still around. Don't so much as speak the names of their gods or swear by them. And by all means don't worship or pray to them. Hold tight to GOD, your God, just as you've done up to now. GOD has driven out superpower nations before you. And up to now, no one has been able to stand up to you. Think of it—one of you, single-handedly, putting a thousand on the run! Because GOD is GOD, your God. Because he fights for you, just as he promised you. (Joshua 23:6–10 MSG)

Journal Notes

Journal Notes

The Great Exchange

I bless GOD every chance I get; my lungs expand with his praise. I live and breathe GOD; if things aren't going well, hear this and be happy: Join me in spreading the news; together let's get the word out. GOD met me more than halfway, he freed me from my anxious fears. Look at him; give him your warmest smile. Never hide your feelings from him. When I was desperate, I called out, and GOD got me out of a tight spot.
—Psalm 34:1–6 (MSG)

Praise is the way! It is the way before the storm to prepare for the storm. Give praise in the storm to give you hope until you're out of the storm. Give praise on the other side of the storm to build gratitude for times between storms. Praise is the way!

The best part about serving God is that knowing Him breeds confidence in the idea that no matter what I'm facing, He has my back; He always has my best for me in mind. He wants my victory more than I do. I know this to be true because His Word tells me this in so many examples through so many people in the Bible.

The thing is, you're never going to know that if you keep your Bible on display on bookshelf. You gotta crack it open, read it, write about it, meditate on it, and memorize it.

Life will continually stir up storms. If we don't know Him, we won't know we can count on Him. Are we prepared for our next storm? Praise is the way! We can't praise what we don't know. We must get to know Him, read His Word, and talk to Him. He's always available and ready to lead you.

Pray This

Lord, I commit to You time to get to know You a little better each day. Draw me close to You and teach me who You are to me, who I am to You, and why that matters. Praise is the way! Teach me about You and Your ways. Stir in me a newness like a first love that I can't wait to get to, amen.

Challenge

Read, write, meditate on, and memorize this.

> Come, children, listen closely; I'll give you a lesson in GOD worship. Who out there has a lust for life? Can't wait each day to come upon beauty? Guard your tongue from profanity, and no more lying through your teeth. Turn your back on sin; do something good. Embrace peace—don't let it get away! GOD keeps an eye on his friends, his ears pick up every moan and groan. GOD won't put up with rebels; he'll cull them from the pack. Is anyone crying for help? GOD is listening, ready to rescue you. If your heart is broken, you'll find GOD right there; if you're kicked in the gut, he'll help you catch your breath. Disciples so often get into trouble; still, GOD is there every time. He's your bodyguard, shielding every bone; not even a finger gets broken. The wicked commit slow suicide; they waste their lives hating the good. GOD pays for each slave's freedom; no one who runs to him loses out. (Psalm 34:1–6, 11–22 MSG)

Journal Notes

Journal Notes

The Great Exchange

There is a river whose streams shall make glad the city of God, The holy place of the tabernacle of the Most High. God is in the midst of her, she shall not be moved; God shall help her, just at the break of dawn. The nations raged, the kingdoms were moved; He uttered His voice, the earth melted. The LORD of hosts is with us; The God of Jacob is our refuge. Selah.
—Psalm 46:4–7 (NKJV)

Whenever we see the word *selah* in the Bible, it is a verb meaning "take action here" directive while you're reading. It literally means to stop, ponder, and meditate on what you just read.

Take a moment and break down verses 4–7. For me, that river is symbolic of God's presence in heaven touching my earthly life. God is with me here just as much as He's in heaven preparing my mansion for my arrival. These verses say this to me.

1. I will not be moved.
2. God will help me at the right time.
3. I hear Him say here that the darkness, the chaos cannot survive His presence.
4. I also hear Him say that He is the safest place my mind can find refuge if I choose Him over the darkness and chaos.

Pray This

Lord, help me remember how to pause and give the words You've left for me to learn about You, and how to put You first, a chance to make a difference in my life here on earth as I allow You to prepare my soul for eternity, amen—selah.

Challenge

Read, write, meditate on, and memorize this: "Be still, and know that I am God; I will be exalted among the nations, I will be exalted in the earth! The LORD of hosts is with us; The God of Jacob is our refuge. Selah" (Psalm 46:10–11 NKJV).

Journal Notes

Journal Notes

The Great Exchange

But there is another urgency before me now. I feel compelled to go to Jerusalem. I'm completely in the dark about what will happen when I get there. I do know that it won't be any picnic, for the Holy Spirit has let me know repeatedly and clearly that there are hard times and imprisonment ahead. But that matters little. What matters most to me is to finish what God started: the job the Master Jesus gave me of letting everyone I meet know all about this incredibly extravagant generosity of God.
—Acts 20:22–24 (MSG)

Paul was speaking in these verses. It's incredible to me how diligent and passionate he was in most every situation. Sometimes, Paul comes off as a little too intense about all this Jesus stuff, but I don't think that's bad. If we know someone's story, his or her intensity makes a little more sense.

Paul, once known as Saul, used to kill followers of Jesus in the name of God until the day the One he used to be against met him on the road to Damascus. That was the day he truly learned how blind he was, how misled he was, and how wrong he was about Jesus and who He was, who He was to Jesus, and why that should matter to him (Acts 9). He was redirected with truth and by truth to share that truth with everyone.

Whom we listen to matters. What and who motivates and influences us matters.

Pray This

Lord, help me see who is motivating me toward Your plan and purpose for my life and whom I am supposed to be influencing toward the plan and purpose You have for their lives, amen.

Challenge

Read, write, meditate on, and memorize this.

> And so this is good-bye. You're not going to see me again, nor I you, you whom I have gone among for so long proclaiming the news of God's inaugurated kingdom. I've done my best for you, given you my all, held back nothing of God's will for you. Now it's up to you. Be on your toes—both for yourselves and your congregation of sheep. The Holy Spirit has put you in charge of these people—God's people they are—to guard and protect them. God himself thought they were worth dying for. (Acts 20:25–28 MSG)

Journal Notes

Journal Notes

The Great Exchange

This is GOD's Word on the subject: "As soon as Babylon's seventy years are up and not a day before, I'll show up and take care of you as I promised and bring you back home. I know what I'm doing. I have it all planned out—plans to take care of you, not abandon you, plans to give you the future you hope for."
—Jeremiah 29:10–11 (MSG)

Seventy years of captivity. Isn't that about the average lifespan of a human these days? Funny how God's Word is so relevant to each generation that experiences it.

I have read these verses hundreds of times for personal prayer and devotional time and to teach others. I have been known to quote Jeremiah 29:11 as my life verse. For the first time, I saw this symbolism of the seventy years of captivity. This is a personal encounter I experienced while studying God's Word to write these forty days of devotions.

In some ways, we are in captivity while we are living this life with a start and an end. This temporary life is a form of captivity. We are captivated by the limitations of time, of bodies that fail us, of relationships that stress us and fail us, and of resources to sustain us. This captivity is accompanied by the assurance of God's presence while we're here and His promise to take us home with Him one day. His captivity is wrapped up in one word: *hope*.

While in captivity, we have hope in Jesus and what He did for us to have eternal life with Him.

Pray This

My hope is in Your presence, and I stand on Your promises, God. I will not make it out of captivity without You, amen.

Challenge

Read, write, meditate on, and memorize this.

> This is GOD's Word on the subject: "As soon as Babylon's seventy years are up and not a day before, I'll show up and take care of you as I promised and bring you back home. I know what I'm doing. I have it all planned out—plans to take care of you, not abandon you, plans to give you the future you hope for." (Jeremiah 29:10–11 MSG)

Personalizing the verses that stick out for you will help you conquer lies and exchange them for truth.

Journal Notes

Journal Notes

The Great Exchange

The Word was first, the Word present to God, God present to the Word. The Word was God, in readiness for God from day one. Everything was created through him; nothing—not one thing!—came into being without him. What came into existence was Life, and the Life was Light to live by. The Life-Light blazed out of the darkness; the darkness couldn't put it out.
—John 1:1–5 (MSG)

Our sweet Jesus is being described here. Reread the verses and let the truth, the reality, the insight into who Jesus is and His power soak in.

He is the Word, the living, breathing, verb of God's written Word. These verses encompass the very motivation behind why getting into God's Word is so important. When we are getting into God's Word, in reality, we are getting into Jesus, our example to live by. Jesus exchanged His body for our sin, but He never sinned.

He is the uncreated One who created every living thing. He became a human for humans, yet He is beyond what the human mind can comprehend. King Jesus stepped out of His perfect heaven for an imperfect people. This is truly the greatest love story ever.

He is the light that leads us out of darkness because darkness cannot put out this Light! Darkness couldn't destroy Him, death couldn't take Him from us, and God couldn't resist sharing this great love with us. When His creation and His beloved Son collided in the greatest exchange of love between the uncreated one, that was Jesus and all creation including you and me saying yes to His proposal. That's salvation.

Pray This

Create in me a desire for You, Lord, that leaves me in a perpetual state of exchanging my sin for Your love, amen.

Challenge

Read, write, meditate on, and memorize this.

> The Life-Light was the real thing: Every person entering Life he brings into Light. He was in the world, the world was there through him, and yet the world didn't even notice. He came to his own people, but they didn't want him. But whoever did want him, who believed he was who he claimed and would do what he said, He made to be their true selves, their child-of-God selves. These are the God-begotten, not blood-begotten, not flesh-begotten, not sex-begotten. The Word became flesh and blood and moved into the neighborhood. We saw the glory with our own eyes, the one-of-a-kind glory, like Father, like Son, Generous inside and out, true from start to finish. (John 1:9–14 MSG)

Journal Notes

Journal Notes

The Great Exchange

So, friends, we can now—without hesitation—walk right up to God, into "the Holy Place." Jesus has cleared the way by the blood of his sacrifice, acting as our priest before God. The "curtain" into God's presence is his body.
—Hebrews 10:19–21 (MSG)

God is available night and day as well as wherever we go and regardless of what we've done. He's way more accessible than we give Him credit for.

If Satan, the devil, the enemy—whatever you want to call the one who always works against God's plan and purpose for our lives—can convince you that dark is stronger than light, that you are alone, that no one cares about you, and that your version of broken cannot be repaired or useful again, he gains a hold on your life. He then has full access to steer you away from God. But the enemy has only as much power, control, and hold on you as you allow him to have.

It actually works the same way in your relationship with God except that He is much more of a gentleman about it. He invites you into His presence to build an intimate relationship with you. God's control actually leads to freedom. God's access to you gives you access to the family of God's inheritance. His presence replaces loneliness with His light, which dispels darkness.

Pray This

Lord, I want to take advantage of this access to You there while I contend with this enemy here. Help me learn how to access You and everything connected to You, amen.

Challenge

Read, write, meditate on, and memorize this.

> So let's do it—full of belief, confident that we're presentable inside and out. Let's keep a firm grip on the promises that keep us going. He always keeps his word. Let's see how inventive we can be in encouraging love and helping out, not avoiding worshiping together as some do but spurring each other on, especially as we see the big Day approaching.
>
> Remember those early days after you first saw the light? Those were the hard times! Kicked around in public, targets of every kind of abuse—some days it was you, other days your friends. If some friends went to prison, you stuck by them. If some enemies broke in and seized your goods, you let them go with a smile, knowing they couldn't touch your real treasure. Nothing they did bothered you, nothing set you back. So don't throw it all away now. You were sure of yourselves then. It's still a sure thing! But you need to stick it out, staying with God's plan so you'll be there for the promised completion. It won't be long now, he's on the way; he'll show up most any minute. But anyone who is right with me thrives on loyal trust; if he cuts and runs, I won't be very happy. But we're not quitters who lose out. Oh, no! We'll stay with it and survive, trusting all the way. (Hebrews 10:22–25, 32–39 MSG)

Journal Notes

Journal Notes

The Great Exchange

My dear children, let's not just talk about love—let's practice real love. This is the only way we'll know we're truly living in God's reality. It's also the way to shut down debilitating self-criticism even when there is something to it. God is greater than our worried hearts and knows more about us than we do ourselves.

If we are not continually seeking God's presence, we are missing out on His great exchange of His love for our sin. It's in His presence that we experience His love poured out on us. When we make it a habit to get in His presence, an overflow is naturally created that pours out onto those we come in contact with every day.

Being in His presence is the beginning of loving Him but also the start of loving ourselves, which leads to our sharing that love with others. The greatest exchange we will ever make is letting go of the sins we find ourselves in for the greatest love we will ever know and then sharing that love with others.

Pray This

Lord, help me to be an instrument of love in Your hand that brings me and others into the knowledge and understanding of who You are, who we are to You, and why that matters, amen.

Challenge

Read, write, meditate on, and memorize this.

And friends, once that's taken care of and we're no longer accusing or condemning ourselves, we're bold and free before God! We're able to stretch our hands out and receive what we asked for because we're doing what he said, doing what pleases him. Again, this is God's command: to believe in his personally named Son, Jesus Christ. He told us to love each other, in line with the original command. As we keep his commands, we live deeply and surely in him, and he lives in us. And this is how we experience his deep and abiding presence in us: by the Spirit he gave us. (1 John 3:18–24 MSG)

Printed in the United States
By Bookmasters